iPhone Photography

A Ridiculously Simple Guide to Taking Photos with Your iPhone

Scott La Counte

ANAHEIM, CALIFORNIA

www.RidiculouslySimpleBooks.com

Table of Contents

Disclaimer: *Please note, while every effort has been made to ensure accuracy, this book is not endorsed by Apple, Inc. and should be considered unofficial.*

Introduction

The iPhone sends text messages, makes phone calls, and even surfs the Internet—but who am I kidding?! You don't spend hundreds of dollars on a phone to use it as a phone—you want to take pictures! Lots and lots of pictures.

The newest iPhone camera—or rather cameras since there are three—are a photographer's dream. For an amateur user, simply pointing and tapping the shutter will get amazing shots; but knowing your way around the iPhone camera will help you turn amazing shots into shots that amaze your family and friends, and surprise them when you say it was taken on a phone.

This book (which is based on the iPhone Pro) will show you how the camera works and teach you things you may not know to help you take even better photos.

Ready to get started? Let's go!

[1]
Taking Photos

This chapter will cover:

- Taking photos and videos
- Using the camera lenses
- Using different camera modes

Taking Photos

The Camera app is on your Home screen, but you can also access it from your Lock screen for quick, easy access.

The Camera app is pretty simple to use. First, you should know that the Camera app has two cameras: one on the front and one on the back.

The front camera has typically had a lower resolution and was mostly used for self-portraits; with the iPhone 11 and iPhone Pro, the front camera was upgraded to 12 MP and takes the same pro photos as the back. All the features covered in this section are on both the front- and back-facing cameras with the exception of Time-Lapse and Pano modes.

There are six modes on the camera. When you launch the app, you'll see the different modes at the bottom just above the shutter. Use your finger to slide to the mode you want; the mode in yellow is the mode that is active.

The six modes are as follows:

- Time-Lapse – Time-lapsed videos
- Slow-Mo – Slow-motion videos
- Video
- Photo (the default mode)

- Portrait – For studio-like photos that give a blurred background effect
- Pano – For panoramic photos

Using the Lenses

The iPhone Pro comes with three lenses:

- Ultra-wide
- Wide
- Telephoto

When you take a normal photo or video (not Portrait or Slo-Mo video) you will see three numbers: .5, 1x, and 2. These represent the lenses. Tapping them will make the preview either zoom in or out.

If you tap and hold one of the numbers, you'll get more precise numbers—so if you don't want to zoom all the way in or out, you don't have to. You can also pinch in and out on your screen to zoom in and out.

What does all this mean in practice? To give you an example, below are three photos taken at the same spot with each lens.

Ultra-Wide (0.5)

Wide (1x)

Telephoto (2)

Different Camera Modes

At the top of the app are three buttons: flash, Night mode, and Live mode. Night mode comes on automatically in low-light settings.

Tapping on the arrow in the middle of this will give you an expanded list of options.

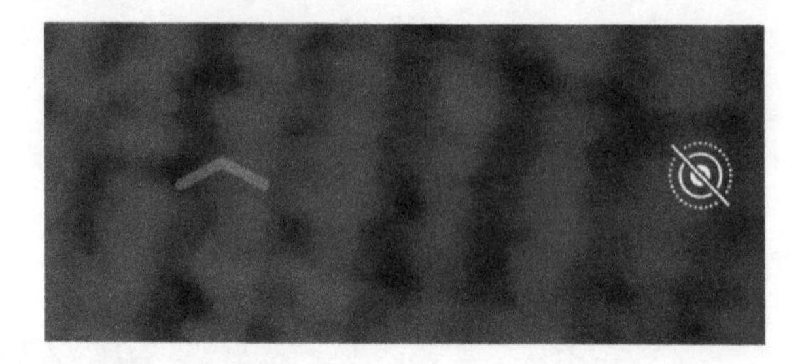

The options appear at the bottom after you expand it. The options are as follows: flash, Night mode, Live mode, frame, timer, and color.

If you tap on any of these options you get more options to either toggle them on and off or, when applicable, make adjustments to them.

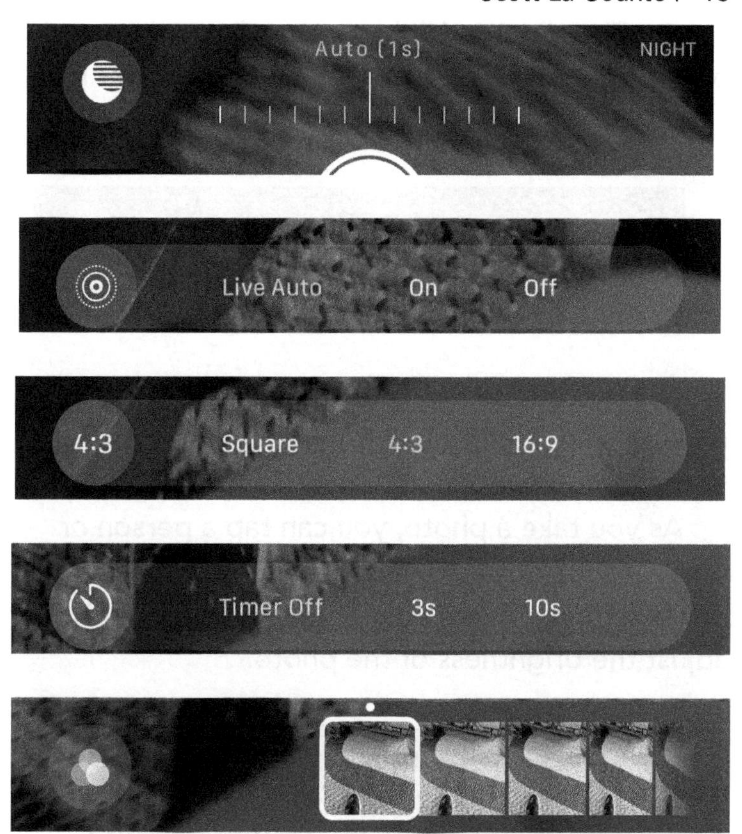

Night mode is a new feature on the iPhone 11 and Pro, and the manual controls here might seem a little unfamiliar; Night mode will come on automatically (if activated, the icon will be yellow and indicate the number of seconds it will shoot for), but when you press the Night mode icon, you can manually adjust the settings it would automatically capture.

What Night mode is doing automatically behind the scenes is simulating a longer exposure. That basically means it's taking longer to capture the image. The slider in Night mode adjusts the number of seconds it will be exposed—the longer it's exposed, the more light you are letting in.

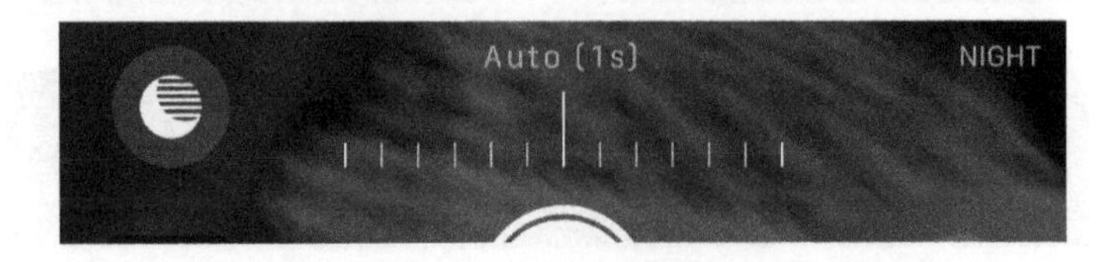

The gyroscope inside your iPhone is smart enough to detect if the iPhone is resting on a tripod. If it is, it will allow for even longer exposures.

As you take a photo, you can tap a person or object to focus on. As you do this, you'll see a yellow box. If you move your finger up or down, it will adjust the brightness of the photo.

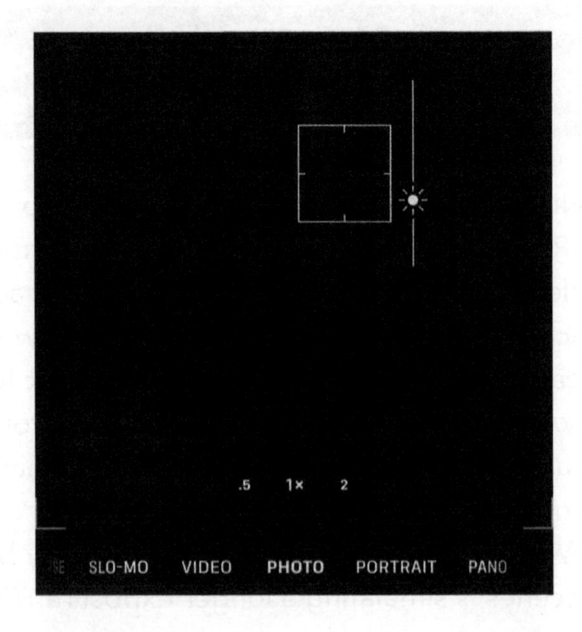

As you take photos, you can capture quick videos without leaving the photo. Tap and hold the shutter and drag it to the right, then release it when you are done recording the quick video. This effect can also be performed when you are shooting a video and want a quick photo.

Burst Mode

Previous iPhones let you take a "burst" of photos by holding the shutter; this was ideal for things like action shots—you could take dozens of photos in seconds and then later pick the one you like best.

Holding the shutter now lets you slide to take a quick video. Burst, however, can still be accomplished. The new method is tapping the shutter and sliding your finger to the left.

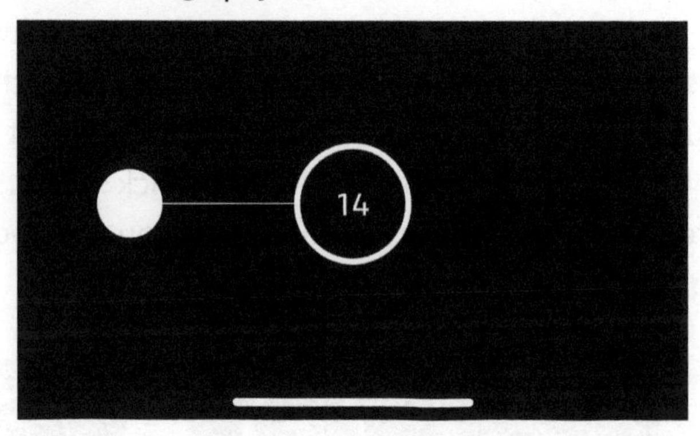

Portrait Mode

One of the most popular camera modes is Portrait mode. Portrait mode captures images that really pop by blurring everything but the subject.

When you drag your finger over the boxes just above Portrait, you can see all the different modes within Portrait mode. They are: Natural Light, Studio Light, Contour Light, Stage Light, Stage Light Mono, and High-Key Light Mono.

When you take a Portrait photo, you can change the mode when you edit the photo. So, for example, if you take it with Studio Light, but decide later that you want Natural Light, it won't be too late to change it. I'll cover this in the next section.

Pano Mode

Pano mode lets you patch several photos together to create one giant landscape photo. You can switch lenses before taking the photo.

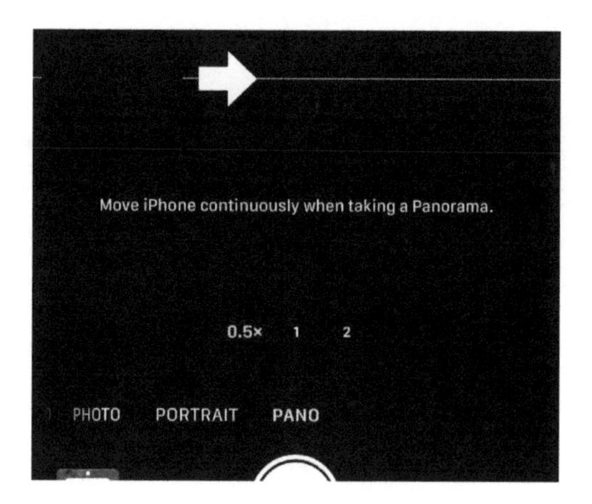

QR Codes

Have you ever seen one of those boxes on a business telling you to scan it for more information? That's a QR Code.

In the past, you would need an app to open that. iPhone's native camera now has that function built in. Hold up your phone to a QR Code and act like you are going to take a picture. As soon as it focuses on it, a drop-down notification will appear asking you if you'd like to open the link in Safari.

[2]
EDITING PHOTOS

This chapter will cover:

- Editing regular and Live photos
- Editing Portrait photos
- Camera settings

EDITING PHOTOS

Now that you've captured your masterpiece, you'll want to edit it to really make it shine. There are thousands of photo editor apps on the App Store. Some, like Adobe Lightroom, will let you make professional changes to the photos, while others are just for fun.

For this chapter, I'm going to stick to making basic edits with Apple's built-in editor. This isn't to say the edits won't be professional—or even fun; there's a lot you can do with the editor.

Regular and Live Photos

The options in editor change based on the kind of photo you took. If you took a Live photo, then there will be a few extra edits you can do; the same is true if you captured in Portrait mode. This first section is going to cover the most common photos: regular (non-Live) and Live.

How do you know what kind of photo it is? When you go into the Photos app and view the photo, it will tell you right below the back arrow in the upper left corner. The below example is a Live photo.

At the bottom of the photo is a list of all options available for editing the photo. The first is the Export button. This option lets you alter the photo outside of the photo app. What does that mean? For starters, you can share via text, email, AirDrop, or upload it to another app, but there's a lot more you can do here: print, add to wallpaper, add to an album, assign to a contact, and more. The next option is the favorite button (I'll cover where these photos go in the next section); the last options are to Edit and Delete the photo.

When you select Edit, you'll see several new options on the bottom in the Now Open photo editor. The first option is the Live button (if it's a Live photo). When you take a Live photo, you'll have several photos within that photo; by tapping on the Live button, you can select the photo you want to use. The phone automatically picks what it believes is the best photo, but this isn't always the case.

Next to the Live button is the option to make corrections to the photo's overall look. The first option is to Autocorrect (this adjusts the lighting and color levels to what the phone believes is best). Next to that are all the manual corrections: Exposure, Brilliance, Highlights, Shadows, Contrast, Brightness, Black Point, Saturation, Vibrance,

Warmth, Tint, Sharpness, Definition, Noise Reduction, and Vignette.

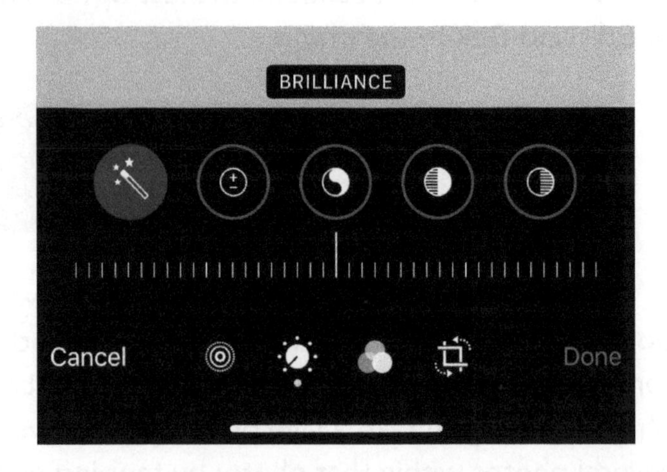

As you slide your finger to the correction you want to perform, you'll notice a slider bar beneath it; you use your finger to move left and right to define the intensity of the correction.

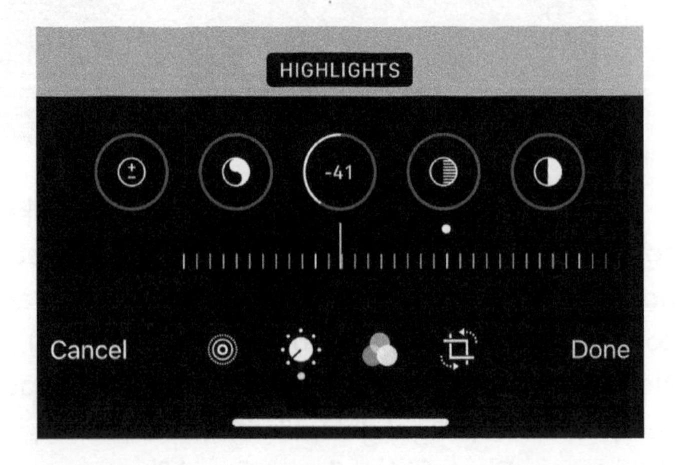

Next is the option to apply Filters to the photos. This works in a similar way: select the filter you want to apply, and then use the slider below to increase or decrease the intensity of the filter. The available filters are Vivid, Vivid Warm, Vivid Cool, Dramatic, Dramatic Warm, Dramatic Cool, Mono, Silvertone, and Noir.

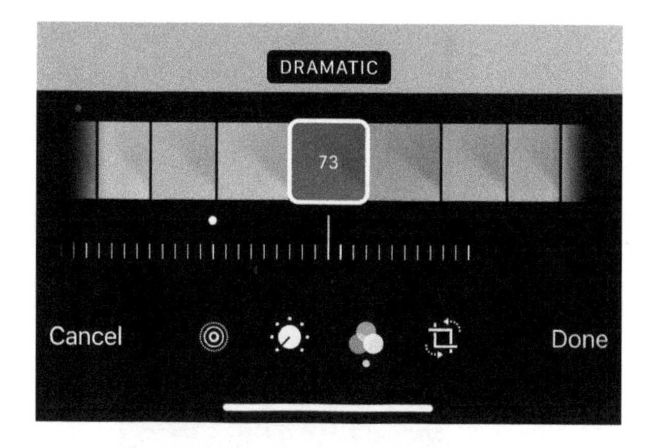

The last option is to Crop. Notice, when you select this option, there are small, white, corner lines around the photo? You can use these to drag to the areas you want to crop—slide in and out, up and down, or left and right.

At the bottom of the cropped area are options to straighten the photo.

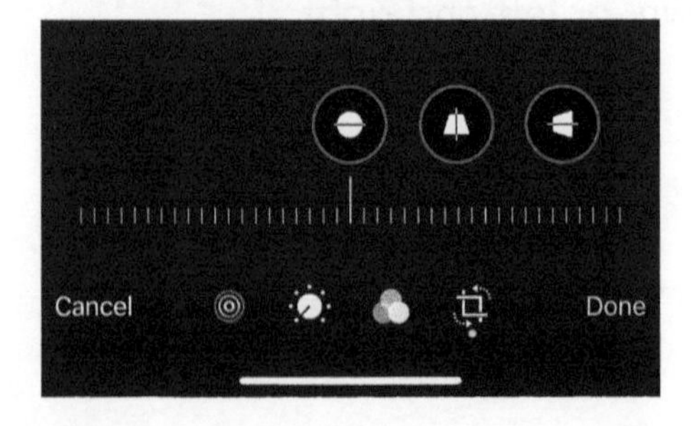

In the top left corner are options to rotate or flip the photo.

The top right has options to crop to a pre-defined size.

When you select the pre-defined size button, you'll see several new options; these are helpful if you are creating for something in particular—like a frame.

When you finish all your edits, tap the Done button; additionally, you can undo everything and keep the original photo by selecting Cancel.

At any point, you can also tap the three dots in the upper right corner of the screen. This brings up the options menu.

If you have other photo apps, you might see them here; the option most people will likely use, however, is the Markup option.

Markup lets you draw and add shapes to the photo—think of it like note taking on a photo.

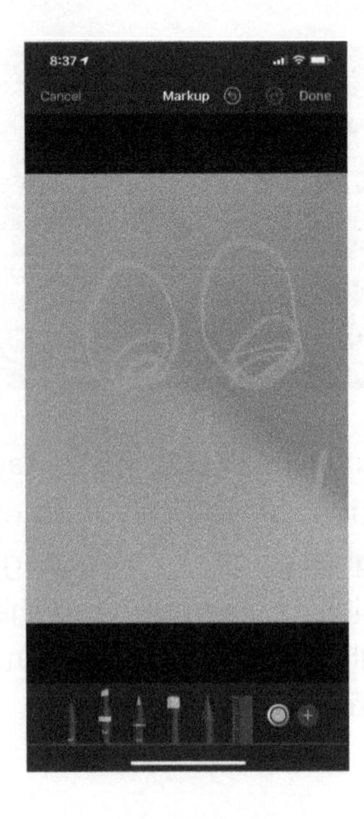

The bottom has all your choices for color and writing instruments. You can also use the ruler to help you draw a straight line with any of those choices.

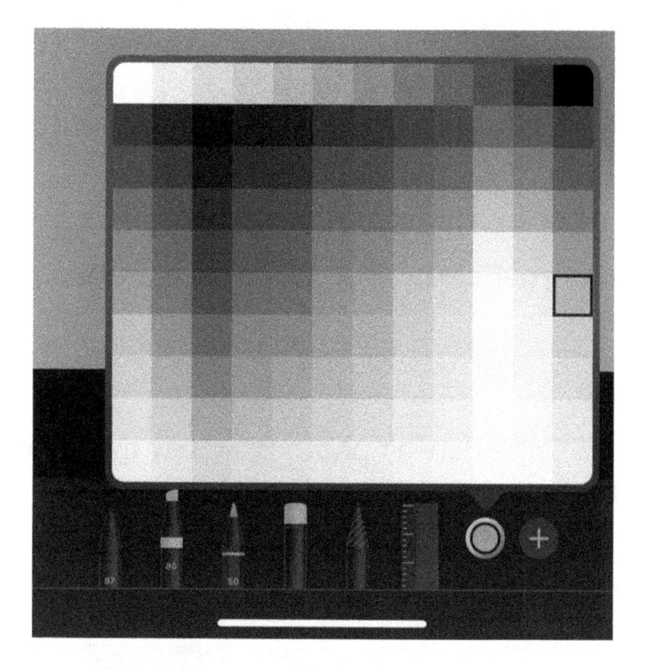

You can additionally tap the '+' button to add shapes, text, a signature, and more.

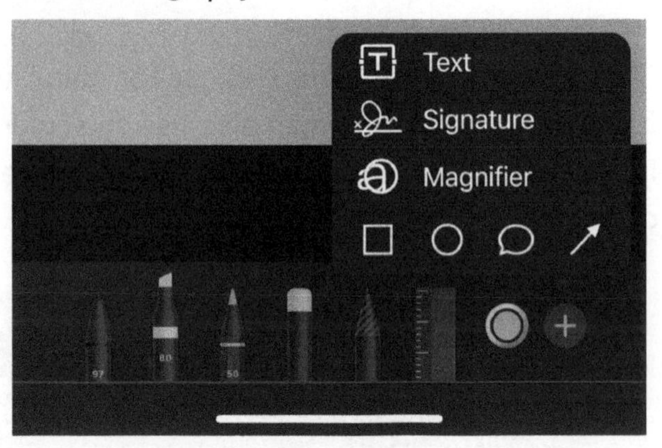

Once you're done with the Markups, tap Done to save your creation or Cancel to erase everything.

Portrait Photos

Editing a Portrait photo is exactly the same—with a few exceptions covered in this section.

You know it's a Portrait photo by the indication at the top of the photo.

Once you tap that you want to edit the photo, select the first button, which brings up the Portrait edits available. Use your finger to slide to the Portrait edit you want to make to the photo. Available filters are Natural Light, Studio Light, Contour Light, Stage Light, Stage Light Mono, and High-Key

Light Mono. Once you make the filter selection, a slider appears below it to adjust the intensity of it.

In the upper left corner of the screen, you'll see a button that says f 4.5; this option adjusts the depth of the photo (or the background blur).

When you tap this option, you'll see a slider appear at the bottom of your screen where you can adjust the depth of the photo.

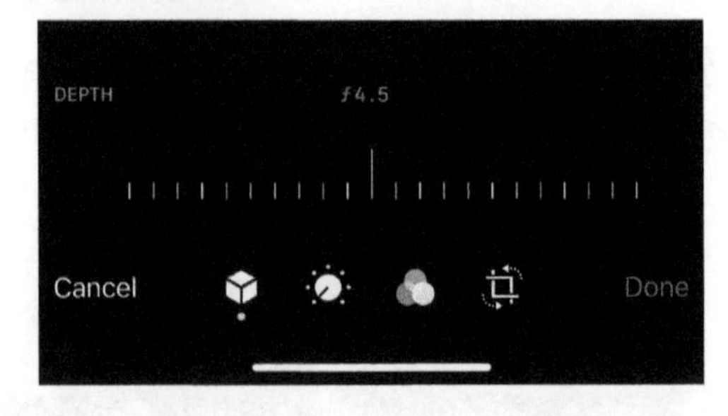

CAMERA SETTINGS YOU SHOULD KNOW

If you go into you Settings, then Camera, there are several settings you should know about (even if you decide not to use them right now).

The setting that I believe is most useful is Composition. Toggling on Photos Capture Outside the Frame means when you take a photo, you can capture more than what you see when you thumb through all of your photos.

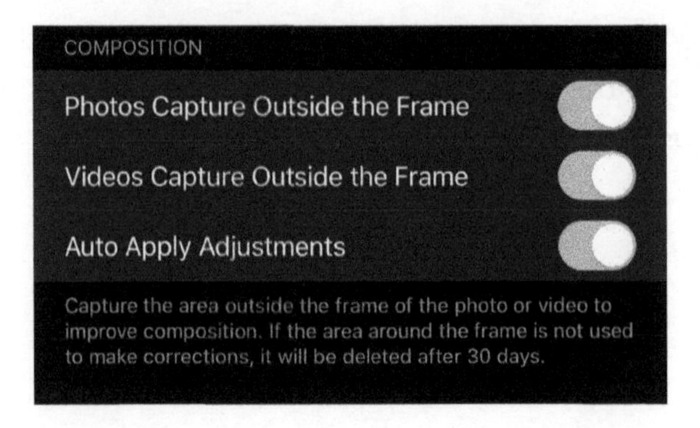

What does that mean? Look at the image below. The image in the center is what I see in my library, but when I go to Edit and Crop, notice how the area is larger? I can drag over to show even more of the photo.

If you don't like that the camera goes back to the default settings whenever you open it, then you can toggle on the Preserve Settings.

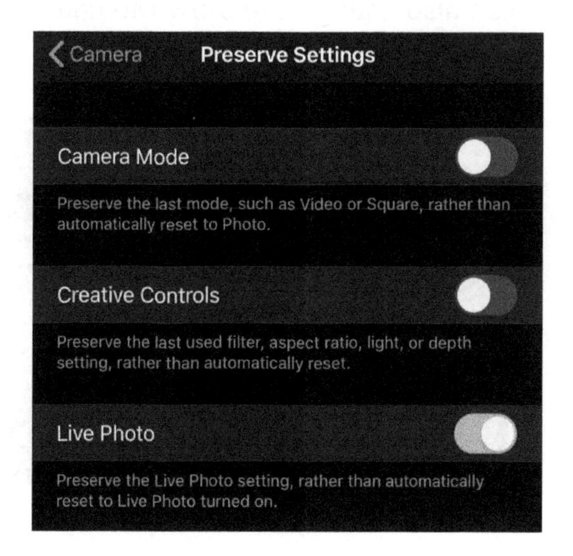

When you record a video, you can shoot as high as 4K. However, doing so creates very large videos. You can record in a lower setting. Tap on Record Video to update your preferences.

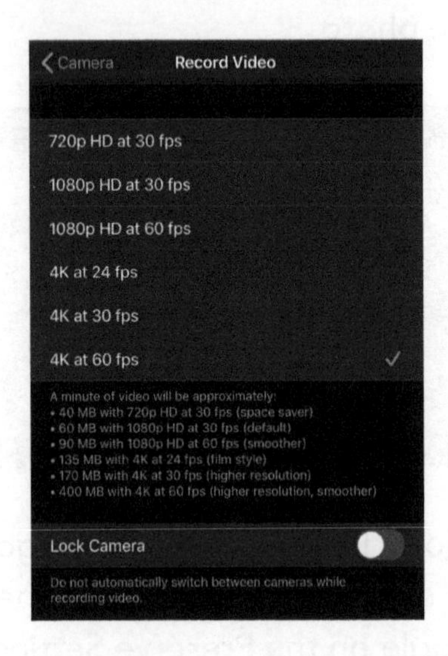

You can also change the Slow-Mo camera settings.

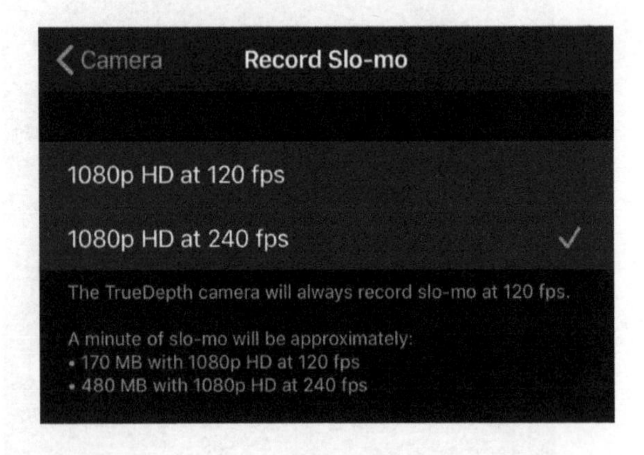

Finally, toggling on Grid will put a grid over your photo app to help you take straight photos and videos.

[3]
ORGANIZING PHOTOS

This chapter will cover:

- Viewing photos
- Sharing photos
- Creating albums
- Searching photos

VIEWING, ORGANIZING, SEARCHING AND SHARING PHOTOS

Now that you have made changes to your photos, how do you find and organize them? This section will cover that.

When you open the Photos app, there are four tabs available: Photos (where you see all photos), For You (curated collections of photos—like On This Day memories), Albums (where private and shared albums live), Search (where you search for your photos).

Viewing Photos

When you select the first tab (Photos) you'll notice a new option appears at the bottom: Years, Months, Days, All Photos. If you are like most people, you probably have thousands and thousands of photos on your phone. This just makes it easier to find what you are looking for.

It also makes it easier to share memories. For example, if I want to share all the photos I took on New Year's Day with my wife, I just go to Years, and go to the year I want, then slide to Months, and find January. Slide again to Days and find January First, and finally in the top right corner tap the tree dots to bring up the options for the photos. This collects all the photos together and gives me a few options: share them, put them in a movie, or show them on a map.

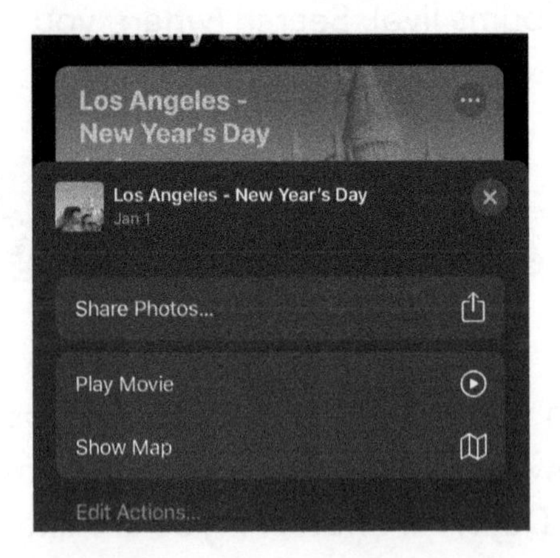

When I select Share, it asks me how I want to share them, and I just pick Messages to text my wife the pictures.

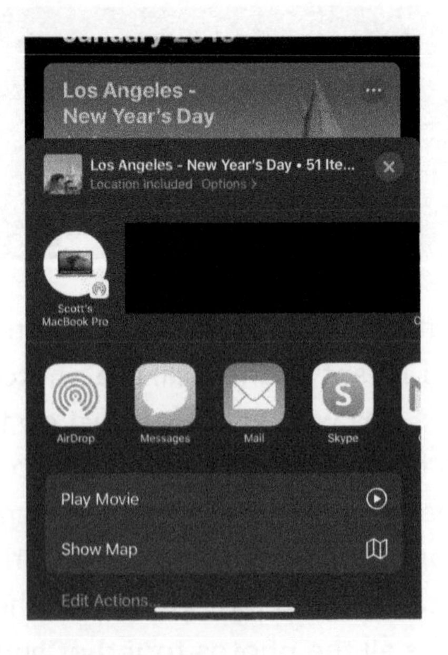

From here, they are all assigned an iCloud link, and that link is inserted into a text message. When my wife gets it, she won't see fifty-one photos appear; she'll see a photo with a link to the location for all. That way she can either view them, download them, or select only a few photos to download.

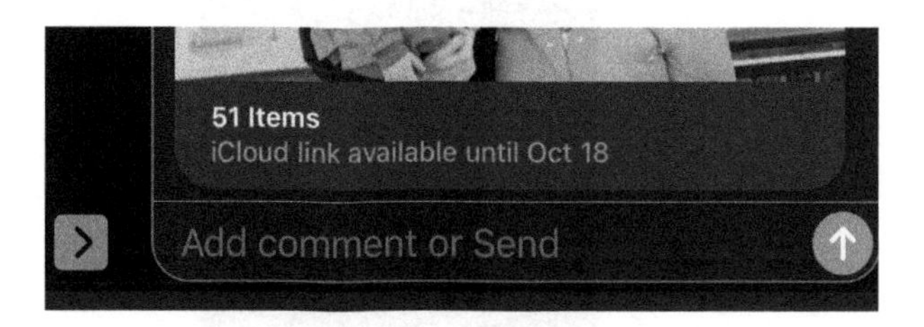

For You

You probably noticed by now that your phone is pretty smart. It has all sorts of things running in the background to figure out who you are and what you like; For You is one area that shows this off. It recognizes when you take a lot of photos in a particular area and marks them as memories, then starts assigning them to this section. You can do all the things you did in Photos, such as share them and turn them into movies.

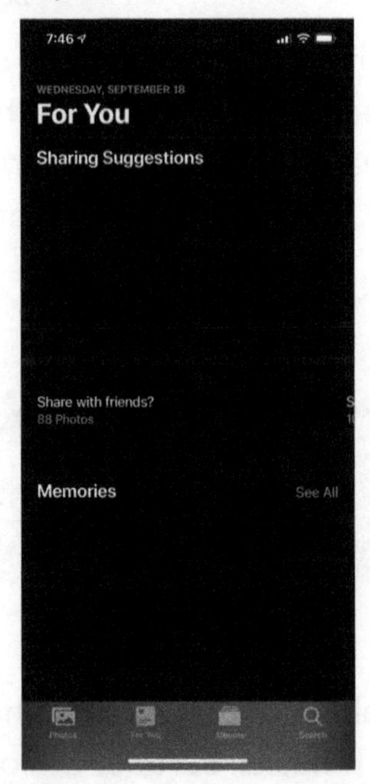

Not all memories are happy ones; when you open up Memories, you can tap the options in the upper right corner to either block or delete a memory.

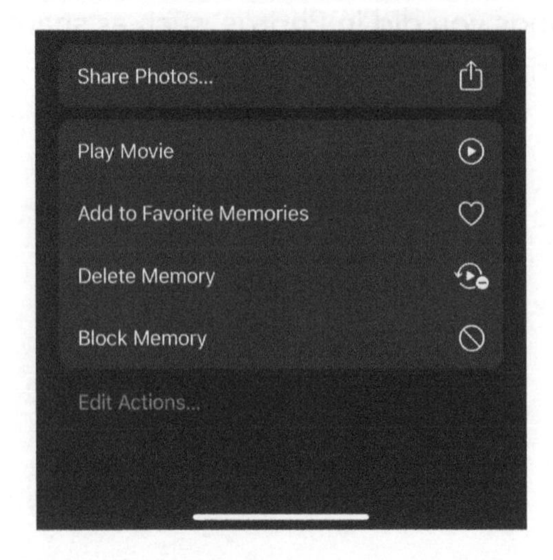

If you decide to play a movie with the memory (and this also applies to any album you turn into a movie), you can edit how it will show—a short or medium clip, and what kind of effects (like music) it has.

Albums

Albums is where you can really start to organize things. Remember when I said above that when you press the like button on a photo it goes to the Favorites folder. This is where you'll find that folder. To add an album, tap the '**+**' button.

This will ask if you want to create a New Album or New Shared Album; the first option is something you see and the second is something you make available to others.

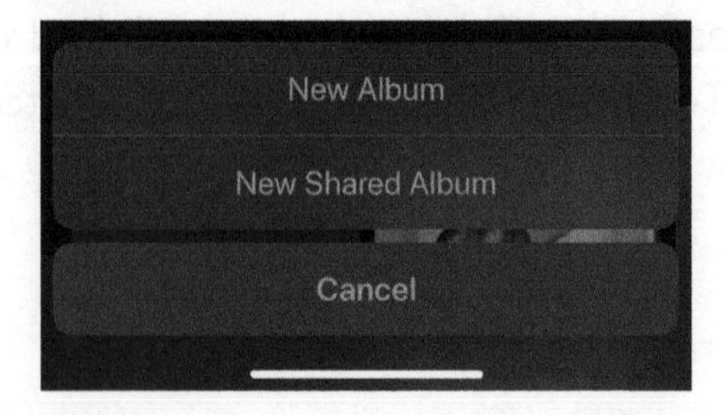

When you create a Shared Album, it will first ask you to give it a name.

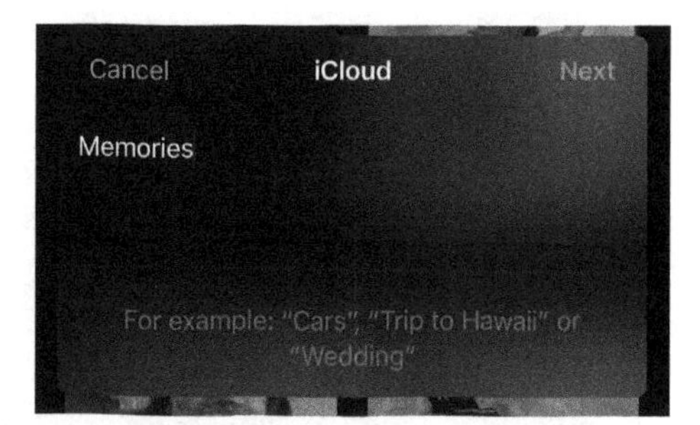

Next, you select who you want to share it with (you can also leave it blank for now).

After this you'll see a blank shared album.

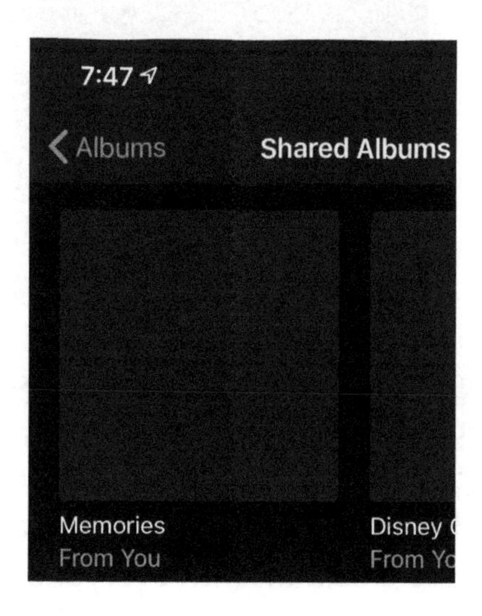

Once you tap on the album, you can start adding your photos.

Selecting People on the bottom allows you to invite people to view it. Under People, you'll also see settings to let people share photos to the album—so, for example, if you just had a wedding, you can share an album with everyone that was there and ask them to add in all of the photos they took. You also go to People to delete an album.

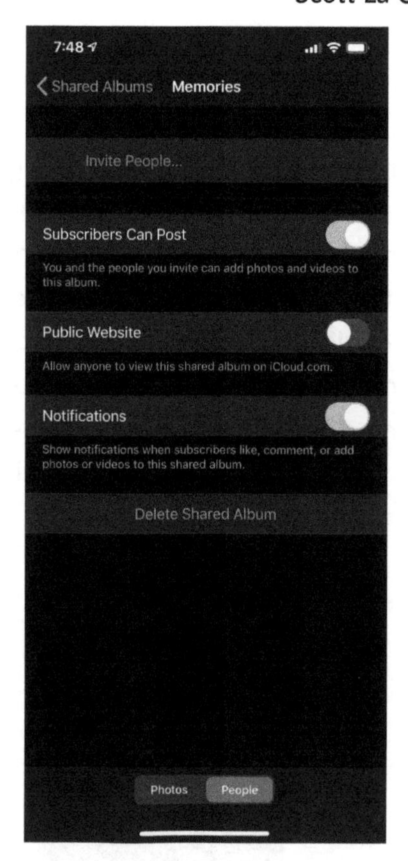

At any time, you can also go into People and tap a person's name who is a member of the album and remove them.

Search

Search is pretty smart. You may wonder how you can search for photos when there is no text. There are a number of ways.

When you take a photo, it geotags the location (in other words, it labels where it was taken—either the city or in some cases the actual name of a place; for example, if you were at a museum, then it would know the name of the museum based on the geotag).

Another way is through facial recognition. When you take a photo, the AI inside your phone scans it to see if it notices a person or even an animal.

One of the first things you see when you tap the search option is People; in the example below, I can tap on Dad and see all the photos I've taken that have my dad in them; I can also search in the box above for a location and Dad, which would find any photo of my dad at that location.

To give you an example, I go to Disneyland a lot because I live in Southern California and have a kid. When I search Disneyland, it will show me every photo I've taken there—over 6,000! Like I said, I go there a lot.

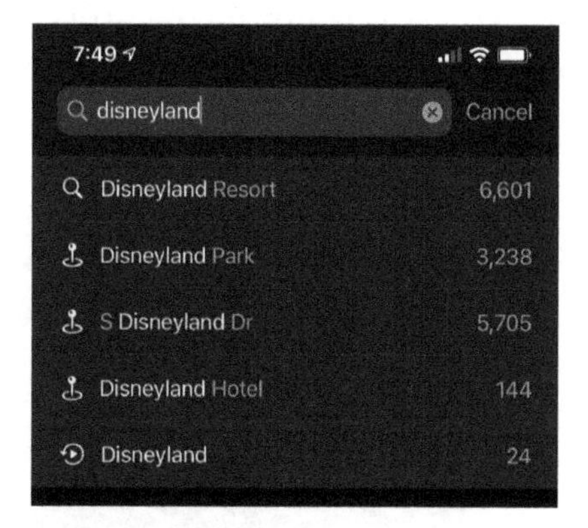

Because there are so many results, I can start adding other things to the search. For example, I can search for Nashville, and then I can also search for just photos with food in them, or just photos taken in the winter.

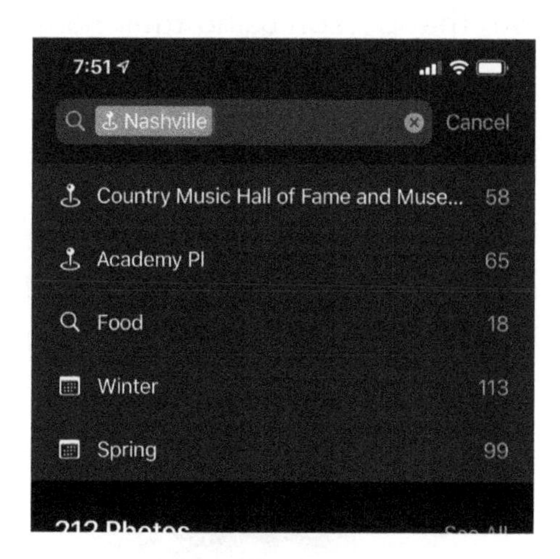

The search isn't quite as smart when it comes to other things, but it's evolving. It can detect objects, for example, but not quite as accurately as people. It does do a pretty good job with animals, however.

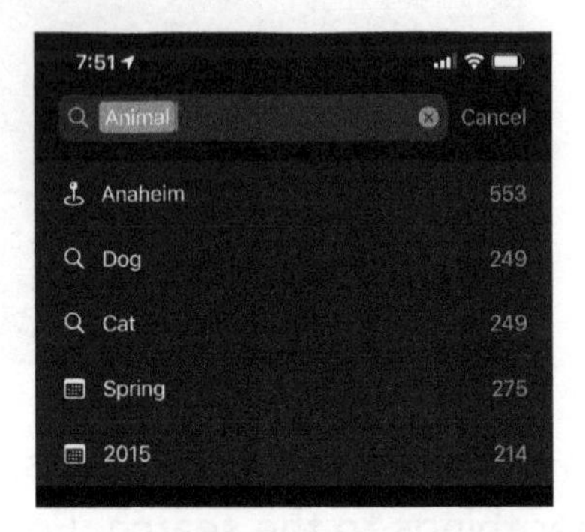

When there is a person it notices in a lot of your photos, it will come up as Unnamed Person; once you give the person a name, it will start showing all photos with that person using their name.

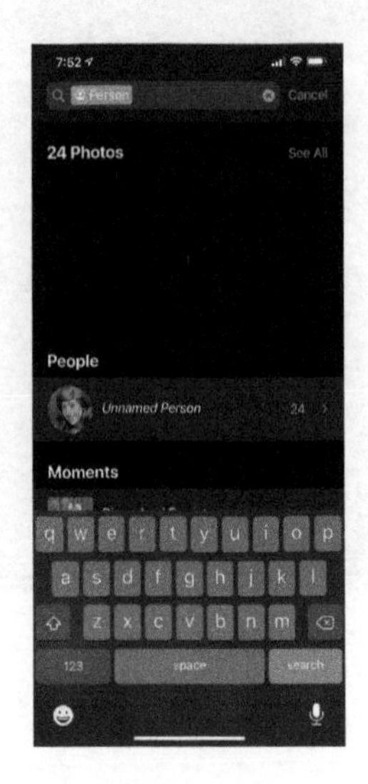

When you tap on a person, you can select the options in the upper right corner to see further options; you can share the photos, turn them into a movie, and more. There's also an option to confirm additional photos, which lets you see photos the AI might not be too sure about.

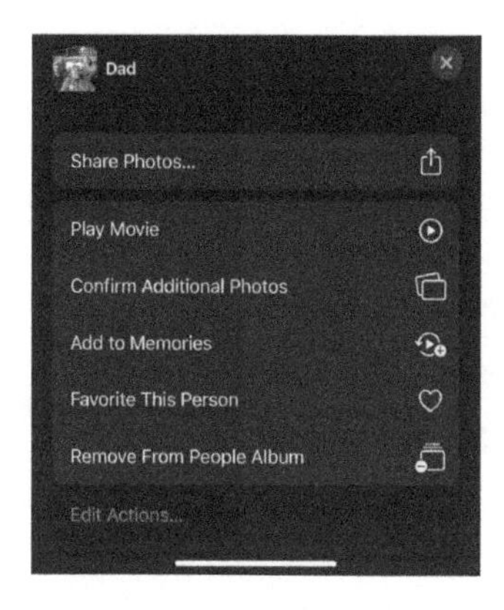

[4]

Mobile Photography Tips

This chapter will cover:

- Photography tips
- Best camera apps

Ready to get the absolute most out of your camera? The tips in this chapter will help!

Know the shortcuts

You can obviously take photos by tapping on the Camera app icon; but finding the app doesn't help when you are in a hurry to take the photo and capture a moment. There are two shortcuts you should know about.

The first is on your Lock screen in the lower right corner. Tap and hold the camera to launch the Camera app without finding it on your Home screen.

The second shortcut is on the icon for the app; instead of tapping to open the app, long press the icon; this will bring up a series of options. It still will open the app, but it will open it right to the mode that you want.

Use your headphones as a shutter

For a few dollars, you can buy a Bluetooth shutter release for your camera. This lets you put your phone on an iPhone tripod (something else you can buy cheap) and take a photo without touching the shutter on your phone. There's an even cheaper solution, however. The headsets that come with your phone double as shutters for your camera. Once you open the Camera app, you can press the volume up on your headset to take a photo.

Use Your Watch as a Shutter

On the subject of shutters, if you have an Apple Watch, you can use your watch as a remote shutter. To use it, open the Camera app on your phone and then open the Camera app on your watch. Your watch now shows what your phone camera sees. If you press the shutter on your watch, it takes the picture on your phone.

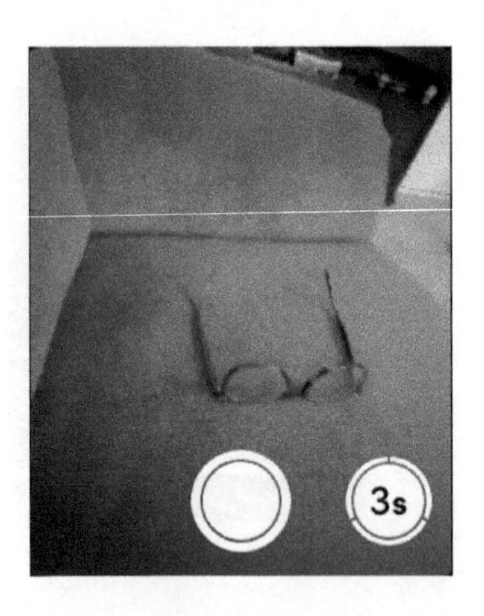

Lighting

Keep the sun behind you.

Make Gold

There is a "best" time to take a photo and it's known as the Golden Hour; it's the time of day that the sun is in the perfect position to give your photos the right lighting needed. The Golden Hour happens twice a day (just after sunrise and before sunset). There are several apps that help you find the Golden Hour where you live, but personally, I find the easiest approach is to just Google it.

To Zoom or Not to Zoom

Don't be fooled into believing your camera has impressive zoom; when you pinch to zoom, you'll see the X's of zooms soaring—but there's two types of zoom: optical zoom and digital zoom. Telephoto zoom means you are using a lens to zoom; digital means you are basically using a computer—or your phone's engine. What the phone is doing is taking a big photo and cropping in. Telephoto zoom can create sharp and close-up photos; digital zoom? It's tricky, but unless you are using a tripod in optimal lighting, then you may not be pleased with the results. Understand your phone's capabilities—when is telephoto zoom reached as you zoom (most likely after 2x), and when does digital zoom start? If zoom is an absolute must for you, then consider investing in a phone lens that you can mount on your phone.

Steady

On the subject of tripods for digital zoom: consider buying one. If you are worried about portability, you can find very small foldable ones (search your online retailer for credit card tripods) or even tripods that fit on your keychain ring.

Flash

Flash can sometimes help an image, but that's not always the case; not only that, leaving your flash on auto can cause your flash to go off accidentally. Personally, I leave it off and turn it on as needed.

What's Your Angle?

Don't settle for a simple point and shoot—experiment with different angles; squat down, for example, and shoot upward from the POV of a dog looking up.

Clean Up

Your camera lens is pretty exposed. Even if you have a good case, things (especially fingers) rub up against it. Clean your lenses with a soft cloth to get rid of unwanted smudges.

Focus

Your phone has a pretty smart auto focus, but don't rely on it; tap where you want the focus to be to ensure you get the shot that you want.

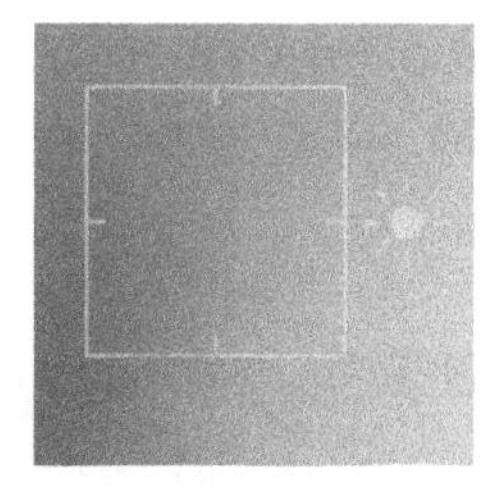

Feeling Exposed?

Similar to auto focus, use manual exposure to make sure your photo is just as bright or dark as you want it before taking the photo; you can slide up or down in the yellow box after you auto focus to adjust the lighting.

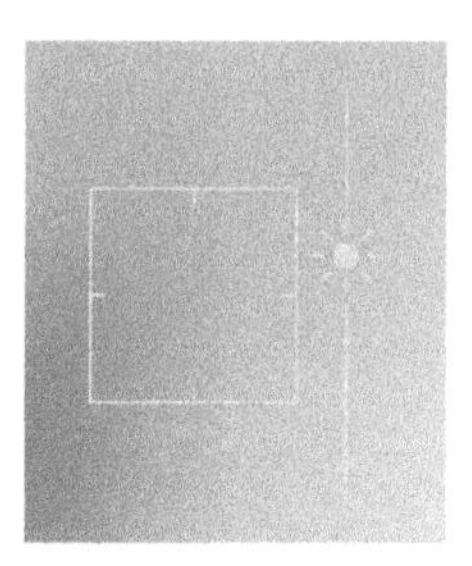

Burst into Action

Use Burst mode for action shots like sporting events to capture just the right shot.

Rule of Thirds

Putting your subject right smack in the center doesn't always create the best photo—in fact, it often doesn't. The rule of thirds is a principal in photography that, in a nutshell, says to put your subject off-center. The best way to use this technique is to go into your camera's settings and toggle the grid on.

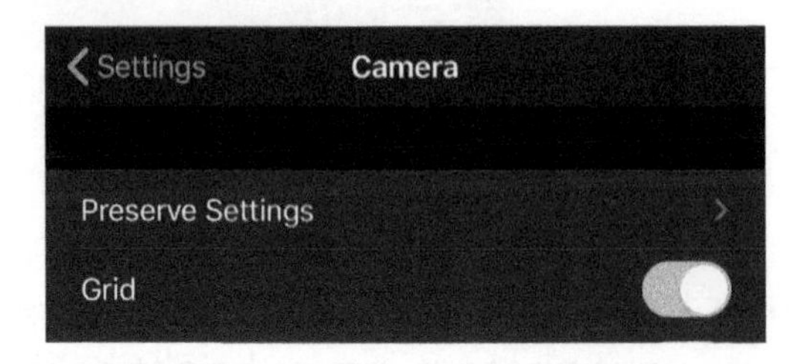

Once it's on, return to your camera and use the grid to position your subject to the three squares on either the right or left.

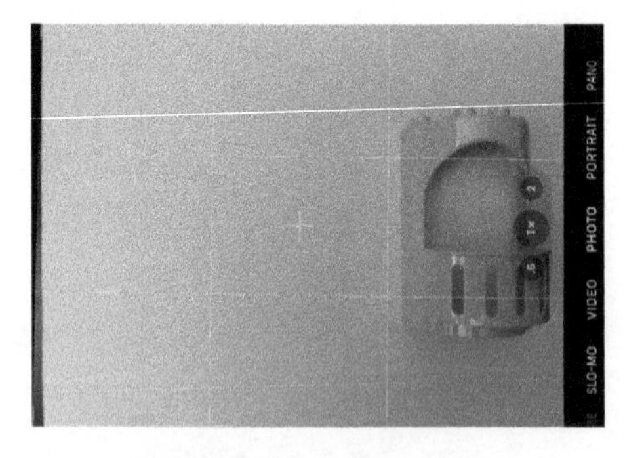

Leading Lines

If you find your photos are flat, then find lines to bring it new life. Lines don't have to be traditional lines that you think of—it could be a tree trunk that leads from the foreground to the focus of your image. In the example below, the leading lines are from the ocean.

Best Camera Apps for iPhone Pro

The point of this book is to help you take better photos on the iPhone's native camera. It's still worth pointing out, however, that there are other options. In addition to hundreds of photo editing apps, there are also plenty of apps that take photos too. Professional and amateur photographers all have their opinions of what is the best pro camera app, but these apps frequently come up—prices for the apps range from about $4.99 to $5.99:

- Halide - In terms of features, Halide has plenty. It has what you'd expect: full manual of things like the shutter speed and ISO, and the ability to export into different image formats such as RAW and TIFF. It also helps you create just the right exposure to really make your images pop.

- ProCam 6 - Over 60 filters and 17 lenses for effects are in this resourceful app.
- Focos - If you just want to try a pro camera app, this is a good one to start with; there's a free download. If you want to try all the pro features, then it's $0.99 a month or $11.99 for lifetime access.
- Moment - Another free app that charges for all features; one thing that separates Moment from other apps is you can buy physical lenses that are designed to work with the app.
- Obscura 2 - You can capture photos in multiple file formats and have access to manual camera functions; once you capture the photo there are over 19 filters available with additional in-app packs also available for purchase.

ABOUT THE AUTHOR

Scott La Counte is a librarian and writer. His first book, *Quiet, Please: Dispatches from a Public Librarian* (Da Capo 2008) was the editor's choice for the Chicago Tribune and a Discovery title for the Los Angeles Times; in 2011, he published the YA book The N00b Warriors, which became a #1 Amazon bestseller; his most recent book is *#OrganicJesus: Finding Your Way to an Unprocessed, GMO-Free Christianity* (Kregel 2016).

He has written dozens of best-selling how-to guides on tech products.

You can connect with him at ScottDouglas.org.

Ingram Content Group UK Ltd.
Milton Keynes UK
UKHW020635290523
422461UK00024B/905